Transgressing Dawn

Meditations on Pain and Power

Treisha

BookLeaf Publishing
India | USA | UK

Made with ❤ on the BookLeaf Publishing Platform
www.bookleafpub.in
www.bookleafpub.com

Dedication

To the ones who learned too late—
that mercy is a mirage,
that betrayal is the oldest law,
that the world does not spare what it cannot wield.

That power is not crowned,
but carved—
into bone.

To those who bled,
not from error,
but because they believed.

At the blade's edge,
in ash's breath,
inside the eye of unmaking—
and did not fall.

Marked by flame—tempered, not tamed.

Preface

The Dawn is a Lie.

This book will not save you.
It will make you strong enough to bear freedom.

It is an altar where the self is unmade—
and something older rises in its place.

These are not lanterns but mausoleums.
Pages where gods have died and myths have rotted.

Do not look for comfort here.
You will only find your own ghost staring back.

If you leave unchanged—
You have read nothing at all.

Acknowledgements

To those who steadied my spine
when it threatened to splinter.

To the ones who didn't spare me
the harrows of truth.

To the silence that shaped me—
to the nights that spit me back whole.

To the ones who stayed.
To the ones who vanished.
To the ghosts I still carry.

You tried to spare me.
But I couldn't take your wisdom.
I had to earn mine.

Through the rite,
I marked myself.
I buried nothing.
Now it wears me differently.

I. Transgressing Dawn

The night takes me as its own—
unmade, unbound, undone.
In its quiet, I dissolve.

A thing without tether. Past. Name.
I slip through the stitches of the world.

The world sleeps.
I stay.
It resets.
I refuse.

I live where the veil thins,
where wounds whisper and silence answers,
where time unspools,
where truth does not beg,
where forgiveness never arrives.

But dawn—
She is a painted mask: hollow, pristine, deceitful.
She binds the clock, seals the wound,
and dares to say: today is not yesterday's ruin.
She lies.

She resets.
She erases.
She buries.

and I refuse—
to belong to the sun.
to greet the morning.

Though she lingers at the edges—
She does not touch me.

II. The Ribs of Night

I do not beckon.
I do not call.
I am not a cipher.

And yet—
you linger.

Fingertips hovering,
breath stilled,
seeking a shimmer,
a fracture in the dark.

Did you think that longing was enough?
Hunger alone cannot bend the dusk.

Some relics crumble beneath desperate touch.
Others endure—until proven worthy.

You stand before something unshaken.
Not waiting. Not wanting.
Just watching.

My fire answers only sacred rites.
It shatters in the hands worthy.

But you—
you have not yet earned the rapture.

This is the art of absence.
The slow, deliberate dance of denial.
The way shadow hums,
but never leans close enough to mark.

So the night swallows its secret,
draws it into its ribs,
folds it into hush.

In the Ribs of Night—
you remain.
Still.
Breathless.
Waiting.

III. Fire and Fog

There is no ease in this.
No gentle unfolding, no casual play.

It is fire meeting fog,
two things never meant to touch,
and yet they do.

Colliding. Combusting.
Vanishing into one hush.

I do not wait to be known.
I do not watch from a distance.

I press my fingers into the edges of knowing,
trace the shape of a thought
until I know the contours like my own.

I see.
And in seeing,
I unravel,
not to shatter,
but to slip through.

There is no haven in this—

no walls to lean upon,
no breath between ruptures.

The ground shifts,
The inhale stills before the strike.

Perhaps that is why it's electric.
Neither of us stay.
Neither of us bow.

When we meet,
it is not out of need,
but out of something rarer—
Truce.

And if this is the last time,
if this is the final waltz,
let it sear—
and vanish without echo.

IV. Michelangelo's Ghost

Her limbs—
Renaissance strokes of wreckage and grace,
as if Michelangelo had painted her
across the domes of churches,
a masterpiece—flawed and exalted.

The movement of her form, a hymn,
a whisper of alabaster against the dark.
I have never seen something so pure—
Never have I witnessed such magnificence—
draped in disarray so divine.

She builds sanctuaries from her own remains,
raises altars to the shadows she has burned,
a divine architect of her own undoing.
Forgotten battles whisper through her bones,
sieges staged inside the sanctum of her mind.

And still—
she rises,
high on the destruction,
a creature of collapse and rebirth,
a body of ruin that does not beg to be saved.

V. Law of Collision

A love where collision is the law.

We mark each other–
Claws in skin.

Not in possession, but in proof–
proof that we touched,
proof that we burned,
that the world narrowed to just this.

We edge toward the death of this power–
but each time, it expands.
A cord runs between us,
unseen. Binding. Pulling.
Never breaking.

You leave imprints in my bones.
press your ghost into the marrow,
etch yourself into the air between us.

Your embrace, and nothing more.
Your body, and everything after.

The joy of tracing you:

the pecks, the pulses, the knowing—
not love, not need,
something unspeakable.

You taste of hunger,
of hands that never beg,
of nights that do not end.

And here, in the velvet hush of you,
I am both sanctuary and the aftermath—
the home that keeps you warm
and the fire that burns you down.

VI. Reverie

What I build, I break.
What I break, I breathe.
I break again.

My skin, cold as the walls I raise—
a hollow sculpt by steady hands.
Wandering its halls, a ghost in my own creation,
adrift from time, severed from what once was mine.

I leave my hands in the clay,
carving until I vanish.
I create. I collapse.
I fracture.

I take what is given.
I waste what is mine.
Nothing is stolen.
I carve my own loss.

I indulge in a feast of my own making—
no shadows dare follow,
no mirrors return my gaze.

The sky fractures, thin as porcelain.

The wind swallows its own howl.
I stand before my detritus,
hands open, mouth silent.
And still, I cannot stop.

You watch.
You wait, as if I will rise again.

VII. Devourer's Creed

The dice had long since been cast.
The hands played before I sat at the table.
And still—I played.
Spellbound by the illusion.

The sleight of hand, the whispered gospel—
that reverence was power,
that surrender dulled the blade,
that those who bled most dined closest to the divine.

They said—
surrender, suffer, bleed,
and you will be made holy.

But devotion—
a dagger, sugar-laced.
A chalice, cloaked in venom.

I bowed.
The cup never touched my lips.
They renamed my hunger into belief.
My ache now an offering.
and called my hollowing divine.

Until starvation soured.
Until famine stung too bitter to bear.

Then—
the mirage split.
The stage collapsed.
The room of worship crumbled to dust.

Monarchs did what monarchs do—
They took.

No laurels for the fallen.
No feast for the sacrificed.

If love ever touched me—
it left no mark.

Only silence.
And the space where praise used to echo.
Only—
the moment I stopped waiting to be spared.

VIII. Wound That Births

I was weaned on silence,
fed to the quiet.
Taught that stillness was survival,
that kindness was currency,
that obedience laid the soft at the altar.

I have seen hands offer too much,
open palms mistaken for tribute,
bodies folded into devotion
to keep the teeth at bay.

But the devouring remains.
There is no virtue in being unscarred.
No reward in being untouched.
The world does not spare the gentle,
but praises the ones who walk into the fire.

To kneel is to be swallowed.
To rise is to threaten.
To master both is madness.
So tell me—
what must one do?

IX. Gatekeeper

I am the gatekeeper of my mind.
No hand turns the lock but mine.
No whisper slips the keyhole.

No prayer bends the iron of my will.
The wind calls— I do not answer.
The tide pulls— I do not waver.

Storms throw themselves at my gates—
they break. They do not enter.
Your words crash like waves,
hungry, breaking, pleading for passage.

I remain stone.
Your fire claws at my door,
licks at the hinges,
melts the walls to gold.

Still, I do not burn.
Nothing binds me to your tide.
No weight of yours will bend my spine.
Feel as you will— that is your own.
What I hold is mine alone.

And should I choose to open,
should I press my key into the dark,
should I let the world step through—
it will be a gift, not a theft.
A power lent, never left.

X. Twisted, The Dawn

I waited. I ached.
I asked the silence if it had left—
but still, I traced the echoes of your voice.

This dawn is twisted.
Fractured between what was given
and what was taken.

The crystals, the chaos,
we unraveled into something raw,
something shimmering, something sharp.

You spilled.
your words bled through my skin,
a confessional carved into the night.

You feared the weight of your own surrender,
but I cradled it,
held it between my teeth like an unholy vow.
Did you know?
Did you see how I folded into your storm,
how I let it consume me,
even as I drowned in the wake?

It stretches pale and indifferent,
I still taste our wreckage,
still feel the ghost of your touch—
a wound that will not close.

In stillness of the morning,
The air carries no absolution.

XI. Kingdom of Defiance

I have stood before water
but did not drink.
Parched–
a beast sculpted by her own refusal.

They would call it folly.
A failure, perhaps,
to those with cupped hands,
offering clarity, offering ease.

But this resistance–
is it madness, or is it worship?
I have played god before.

Mocked the desert and called it kingdom.
Crowned my own famine.
Starved for the pleasure of knowing
the world could never feed me.

Am I important?
I let the silence answer.
And if I must drown,
let it be in a tide of my own making.

Let it drag me under,
Let it hollow,
Let the heavens watch—
and wonder if I will ever give in.

XII. The Gospel of Betrayal

Once, I stood at the precipice,
a child of melancholy,
bruised with envy, watching the clusters of mortals—
feeding off of one another,
bound in their gossamer webs of devotion.

I mistook hunger for holiness.
Mistook my own bleeding for proof that I was worthy.
But no god came.
They said—
surrender, suffer, bleed,
and you will be redeemed.

But **love** is no altar.
It is a **ledger**.
A **weapon** lacquered in affection.
A game played by those who know exactly when to fold.

I was naïve once.
I gave with open hands,
foolish enough to believe that abundance was a gift—
not a death sentence.

They drank from me like thirsty wolves.

And I—
like an ***idiot god***—
let them.
Not out of kindness,
but because I needed to believe
that loyalty meant something.

But betrayal is not an accident.
It is **architecture**.
A decision dressed as inevitability.

They didn't betray me because I failed.
They did it because they could.
Because it cost them nothing.

There are no laurels for the fallen.
No feasts for the sacrificed.
I am ***no longer a supplicant.***
I am ***not the broken thing on the floor.***

I built a citadel from my own bones.
Sharpened its gates with the teeth of the ones who came before.
I no longer beg for loyalty.
I manufacture consequence.

If love costs nothing—

then it is worth nothing.
I do not fester in longing.
I am the thing that is longed for.

And when I take—
I take what cannot be returned.

Let them write me in warnings.
Let them bury my name in salt.
Let them curse—
it was never theirs to bless.

XIII. The Sovereign's Law

They came with bowed heads,
whispers coiling like slow poison—
counsel, they called it. Wisdom, they swore.

But I have seen wisdom rot in the mouths of men
who sought to shape me in their image.
Once, I listened.

And for my listening, I was bound.
For my trust, I was shackled.
For my softness, I was consumed.
So I tore myself free.

Wrenched the chains from my wrists.
Carved a new order into the world.
No council shall rise where I am the subject.

No voice shall temper my fire.
I shall rule here.

Let them weep for what they have lost.
For I, and I alone, remain.
This is the law.
And it is written in the hands that dare not touch me.

XIV. The Procession of Ashes

The night drapes itself in velvet black,
folds of shadow swallowing my name.
No mourners line the gates.
No bell tolls the hour.

Only the wind sings—low, reverent—
as if it knows this is the last requiem.

I walk forward,
feet grazing the dust where my past was buried.

They tell me I should
press my palms to the soil and beg the dead to rest.

The coffin is split open, emptied of ghosts.
The pyre still smolders, licking at the bones
that once dared to bear my name.

A husk of old words curls into smoke,
a scripture unwritten, a prayer revoked.
There is no eulogy.
There is no tether.

Only the sound of my own breath,
a single step forward,
and the silence that follows.
The dead calls,
and I—
I haven't yet answered.

XV. The Last Innocent

Once, I believed innocence was virtue.
That the soft were righteous,
that the ones who bled, never bit,
would inherit the world.

But the world—
It does not slow down for the gentle.
It does not wait for the quiet.
It eats them first.

And what of the hunter?
What of the wolf?
Did the hunter ever mourn the slaughter?
Did he hesitate before the feast?

So tell me—
if innocence is not enough to keep them from the blade,
if the lamb is always to be devoured—

If innocence is the first to die.
Then I refuse the offering.

XVI. The Woman Who Forgot

There was a woman who forgot,
not because she wanted to,
but because ***memory is cruel,***
building rooms that collapse before she can return.

She wishes she had known more,
that wisdom might have let her see the knife before it entered.

She wishes she had measured time with more than regret,
that she could have held it in her hands,
rewritten the chapters she did not mean to live.

But there is no mercy in looking back.
The past does not wait for understanding.
The years do not grant time to decide.

And so she stands—
not in shame—
but in pride.

Because somehow, against the collapse,

we are still here.

Despite what was taken,
despite what was forgotten,
despite what could have been rewritten—

We are still here.
And there are things I will never say.

XVII. Ones Who Walked Beside Me

I do not say your name.
Some things must remain untouched.

But we have walked in the same fire,
worn the same wounds,
stood by the same coffins where mothers wept,
and fathers did not.

We learned, too young,
that trust is a door left unlocked,
that the ones who smile,
who reach out their hands,
can take something
you did not know could be taken.

You have seen what I have seen.
You have taken the hits I did not.
And I—
I, in my selfishness,
let you carry what I should have shared.

And in your silence, I found my measure—
the weight of what I could not carry

became the edge I now wield.

We were children,
and the world made us pray to the wrong gods.
I am sorry.

Not for my existence,
not for my love,
but for the times I mistook your strength
for something endless.

I hope you know
that I meant it—
every thank you,
every silence,
every moment I wished to say more,
but did not.

And though the road pulls us apart,
though we walk alone now,
I still feel the echo of your footsteps beside me.
I do not say your name.
But I hear it,

in the twitch before the strike,
in the hush before sleep,
in the silence I have grown to wear.

XVIII. The Grey of the Eternal

If this is the final descent –

To the chains,
let the poison seep slow
into the marrow of my bones.

They whisper of return, of atonement,
as if fate does not hunger for my ruin,
as if the noose was not already waiting.

If I snuff the embers that bid me burn,
still the pulse, silence the chase—

will I be saved,
or merely sealed inside my own echo,
a relic of a life unlived?

I walk,
a specter in disarray,
a fractal unformed.

Numbers, reason—
trivial weights upon my spirit.

For I am bound by language alone,
a creature of words and whispers.

Madness calls, and I do not flinch.
No gods remain to barter with,
no morality to cradle me.
I have traded my conscience
for the grey of dawn eternal.

The night drips slow,
thick with the scent of jasmine.
Phantoms murmur in silver tongues,
the air dense with something waiting.

A specter beckons—
not with hands,
but with absence.

A door ajar in the dark,
a quiet that hums.

Do I enter? Do I fall?

Laughter spills from my lips,
sharp as shattered glass,
as if I ever had a choice.

I step forward—
a flicker, a fracture,
suspended in the breathless space
between ascent and freefall.

No gravity, only motion.
No weight, only flight.

XIX. The Fractured Divine

Grieve over me like a glitch,
an **aberration** in the grand design,
a **fracture** in the etching of fate.

For thy grooves,
in the **futility of nuance,**
my muse bleeds—
a lament for my glory,
a **requiem for my ruin.**

I am the child of otherworldly gods,
woven between realms,
a **hymn, forbidden.**

Misinterpret me at your peril,
for the cost of misunderstanding
is a fortune **you cannot afford.**

Remedy your tyranny,
for when I step toward you,
the **ground shifts,**
the **world shatters,**
and you—

you **surrender**
to the **magnificence of vision,**
to the unmaking of certainty,
to the **dark that does not destroy,**
but transforms.

XX. Crown of Silence

No Whispers.
No Ghosts.
No Gods.

The silence does not haunt me.

It does not beckon,
does not breathe.
It does not ask if I am afraid.

It is not eerie.
It is not comfort.
It simply **is.**

I have stripped the world of sound,
bled the echoes dry,
made **stillness** my dominion.

Once, the silence gnawed.
Once, it clawed at the edges,
a hunger with no mouth.

A **throne, hollow**—
no prayers, no pleas.

I have made this silence.
I have **crowned** it.
And it will not move.

XXI. The Final Transgression

You will try to reach the end.
But you have already arrived.

The sentence waits—
but the **silence waits longer.**
A step ahead,
a step behind.

A door that was never there,
a passage already forgotten.

You want to finish this.
You want to **unwrite** it.

You want to walk away,
but the **pages do not turn back.**
You want to be released.
You want to dissolve.

You want to stop reading.
But the **book does not stop.**

There is no last line.

No closing of the gates.

No release,
no crescendo.
Only **motion**, only breath,
only the **hush before the abyss hums.**

Only the pause before you realize—
you are still inside.

Everything here will move you.
Everything here will **still** you.

You do not own this ending.
You do not escape this fate.

Do not hold.
Do not let go.
Only **listen.**
Only **linger.**

And when you turn the final page—
you will not know if you have left.